This Small Machine of Prayer

This Small Machine of Prayer

Poems by

Beth Gordon

Cover design by Shay Culligan

Cover art by Elise Rothenhoefer

ISBN: 978-1-954353-94-7

Kelsay Books
502 South 1040 East, A-119
American Fork, Utah, 84003
Kelsaybooks.com

for my parents, Sidney and Gloria
your love is in every word

Acknowledgments

These poems or earlier versions of these poems were first published in the following journals:

Anti-Heroin Chic: "Tuesday Night, Unarmed"
Barren Magazine: "The Weekend We Ate Curry"
Burning House Press: "Season Thirteen: Episode Twenty-Four"
Califragile: "Who's Keeping Track of Our Dreams," "Elegy with Scrambled Eggs," "Ours Was a Softer Kind of Landing," "Inside Out Abecedarian"
Coastal Shelf: "Safety Information on the Card Located in the Seat in Front of You"
EcoTheo: "If You See Something Say Something"
Everything in Aspic: "If You Are Unable or Unwilling to Perform These Functions," "The Nearest Exit May Be Behind You," "Remove Your Shoes and Place Them Directly on the X-Ray Machine," "Seat Backs and Tray Tables Must Be Returned to Their Upright Position," "Place All Items Larger Than a Cell Phone in a Separate Bin"
Five:2:One: "I Am Moderately Sure of the Nature of Reality"
Free Lit: "All Passengers Must Carry Their Own Boarding Pass"
Hunger: "A Water Evacuation Is Also Unlikely," "The Plastic Bag Will Not Fully Inflate"
In Between Hangovers: "Fortune Teller"
Into the Void: "Elegy with Cover Band," "In Which I Compare My Monolingualism to Una Puerta"
Juke Joint: "Please Report All Unattended Bags or Packages," "Samsonite Sonnets"
Menacing Hedge: "Sprouting Grass & Fish & Egg," "Elegy with Frankenstein"
Morning Walk With Dead Possum, Breakfast and Parallel Universe (Animal Heart Press): "I've Been Dead Since the Beginning," "The Longest Day, 2018"
Open: JA&L: "Apollo 11," "I Paint Your Portrait But, on the Canvas, A Library"

Particularly Dangerous Situations (Clare Songbird Publishing House): "The Possibility of Journey is a Heavy Thing"

Passages North: "Elegy with Flying Tires"

Pidgeonholes: "Items May Shift During Takeoff"

Poetry Breakfast: "Category 4"

Pretty Owl Poetry: "Efforts to Reintroduce Red Wolves Were Unsuccessful"

Quail Bell: "In Which I Refuse to Write a Poem on What Should Have Been Your Sixth Birthday"

RHINO: "Tea Leaves and AI"

SETU: "In Which I Contemplate Drowning in the 3rd Oldest River on Earth"

Slink Chunk Press: "We Know You Have a Choice in Airlines"

SWWIM: "21st Century Omniverse Sonnet," "In Which I Am Surprised to Find Myself in April Again"

Trigger Fish: "In the Event of a Loss of Cabin Pressure"

Viola Vox: "The Things You Survived Before You Were Born," "To Start the Flow of Oxygen Pull the Mask Towards You," "Summer Solstice Eve 2019," "In Which We Are Very Selfish Birds"

Yes Poetry: "Hungover Sonnet: Valentine's Day"

Contents

This Small Machine of Flight

Supplication

Orison

Invocation

Elegy with Flying Tires

When I say tree, I mean your serious
eyes covered by last year's pennies, I mean
mulberries dropping like rotted angels,
gray wood transformed into impressionist
still life, I mean thunderstorm warnings wrapped
in incense ash, I mean the way we say
warm blanket and no one questions or asks
for cold water, I mean Stephen Hawking's
voice as dead cosmonaut, his robotic
words heard by billions and yours heard only
by God. When I say God, I mean earth worm,
the way I dream your smell, half dragonfly,
half sea otter, I mean I cannot draw
your face without lily pads and every
shade of green, I mean I believe in your
existence without elbows or carved stone
or morning, I mean tires that escaped
and murdered a student on her way home
from her sister's wedding, I mean all things
that happen on a Wednesday afternoon.

Sprouting Grass & Fish & Egg

There are un-resuscitated children waiting to glide into sweet crocodile lives where they will swallow catfish and frog colonies, float in happy swamps, digest heron spines and beaks, the mysterious source of their terminal malfunction soon forgotten, like quarantined medical scraps: follow the trail of ash, of fossil to this moment in the story. I was

      thinking of Charles today, bone-mending

friend to my daughter, of Danielle's purple shoes, her laugh so loud that its endless howl remains, Adrienne I was thinking of you, of your trampoline heart, of the caged hamsters and snakes my children loved and lost, of my living grandchildren, their tadpole skin, of their sister's hand pressed into rock, sweet lives returning to the journey's source.

*

Silver-haired translator of reptile songs,
of hearts beating inside flesh that requires
a light source to continue the journey.
I have sucked bruised-plum marrow from bone, raged
to crimson butterflies that I am not
afraid of death's remains, my fingers dipped
in sweet brown ink and placed, like a feather,
on a train's metal canvas, so I can
re-create their faces while you remove
your shoes, listen to tree bones in the fire.

*

The pink phlox found their moon tonight, sprouting moon, moon to
startle hibernating frogs and in that glow I see the living, the way
they beckon me, my children with their cigarettes, defying death
with every breath, howling at ash, their hearts etched with each hard
step of the journey, like fossils caged inside ribs, painting the faces
of daughters and sons, nieces and

    nephews with crocodile ink so the reaper passes close

but does not blink. My mother's father spent his final days stalking
oxygen, he was the first to go, then my father's mother, her sharp
heron smile: my hopes evaporated like a vampire child in sunlight.
My mother's mother still remains like purple-plum flower dust in a
rusted soap can beneath my bed with boxes of color.

*

Crimson and sweet brown, reptile white, catfish
gray, she gathered her bones and walked away
singing resurrection hymns. These sweet deaths:
crocheted escapes that left me wilder than
a train, frog songs in my ears. My father's
father, last to go at 96 years,
no need to explain, his life a pure love
story. Grass moon, egg moon, howl to the dead
and light our way, small petals at our feet.

I Am Moderately Sure of the Nature of Reality

I'd buy morphine from you if it didn't require human interaction, reciprocal need, saving your Japanese fighting fish from certain death. Although it's a business transaction, please don't offer me your hand. Just last week another girl lived in your apartment and later she died, took her last breath in the trunk of my car. I've already gotten used to the idea of you not being here. My doctor's voice is a wasted echo. It's not that I disagree with anything she says. It's just that her glimmers of hope are like goldfish in a piranha tank. She signs the release papers, forges my signature.

Season Thirteen: Episode Twenty-Four

The midnight television hisses reptilian stories of a man whose
son hacked him with an axe, left for dead, but his primal brain,
protected within the myelin sheath, kept him upright and able
to walk to the kitchen, pour a bowl of granola, pack a BLT, celery
stalks and vanilla pudding, spilling blood and crumbs and wilted
lettuce on the slick linoleum floor, walk out the front door that
locked behind him, across dew-dripping grass to collect the damp
newspaper, retrieve a key beneath the stone, before succumbing to
his wounds.

I've seen this episode 10 times or more, and each time that he is
unable to open the orange juice container, or see his reflection in
the bathroom mirror, I wonder if I am dead, if the warm wet sand,
oyster shell fragments, smoldering leaves, beneath my tender feet
are the final gasps of my synaptic gaps and I cannot explain to
even you why this comforts me or why murder by family and
strangers who covet new cars and unscarred skin, is no surprise
to me, the rhythm of bodies rotting in undiscovered graves,
my simplest lullaby.

At 2 am you begin your quiet snoring, asleep in a dream of
blooming poppies, crème brûlée and Mississippi delta jambalaya,
and I will dream of nothing, and tomorrow when I wake in a bed
next to your bed, I will wonder if we are dragonflies in the life
where we hover above lotus blossoms, our unwritten life as old
lovers walking hand in hand into the bay, or that other life where
nobody cuts my throat, leaves me in a watery ditch, the perfect
life where I do not speak of crows or write my own obituary.

Tuesday Night: Unarmed

No amount of incense ash, multi-deck
tarot card predictions or perfect drops
of winter wine will hold you here, the road
your only constant, the road and the way
you always add dark beer and cinnamon
to chili. I write notes in the margins
of all your books, the back of liquor store
receipts, the bottom of the whiskey jar
you will leave behind. I will wash the sheets,
scald them free of your lemon-minted skin,
pretend the days between the days are not
real. Pretend I am the girl in a peach
nightgown stained with coffee, changing from black
shoes to brown, wrapping scarves and necklaces
around my sad throat, rearranging chairs
until I've forgotten where you last sat.

Letter: Summer Solstice 2017

Her cousin was born this week, her mother moved to Florida to work on a cricket farm, and now I stare at photos, scour the internet for stories of rare and violent death, sip red wine and read about the 40 vanishing tribes in Siberia, some with less than a dozen survivors of this strange and modern world where polar bears have no place to rest, a solar eclipse will darken our world in 60 days, petunias cling to life, my failure to provide a proper balance of water and sun is beginning to show, I know the wine is not right for this weather but I'm not going out in this heat and the vodka bottle sits empty in the freezer, my feet are numb, the air conditioner grumbles and watches me search for socks and long-sleeved sweaters on this day in late June, I am appalled at my own audacious suffering, comfortable in my home. How are you, did you get the obituaries I sent?

In Which I Contemplate Drowning in the 3rd Oldest River on Earth

I am a curator of tears, sweetish-
spiced rituals of collect and capture,
barrels and teacups, tissues and trashcans,
invisible syllables discarded
in the crone's well that grandfather first dug
in the ugly winter of ought seven,
when children of seven witnessed raw ice
for the first time in their swamp lives, frozen
water, brutal and pure, that changed the shape
of their hearts. When my upstairs
neighbor showered yesterday he forgot
to pull the barrier curtain inside,
his water crept through my halls, my ceiling
forever scarred with the path of failing
liquid and the maintenance man says wait
for it to dry while I hammer stainless
steel nails, a carpenter in witch's shroud.
I transcribe cracks in my sliding glass door
while it storms as you drive west. I have
everything to say about tears, bring
out the old tin tub, let sun brew the rain,
immerse yourself into that photographed
day before you knew your own sacred name.

Efforts to Reintroduce Red Wolves Were
Unsuccessful

That day I learned I would do anything to be happy. I would
lean into branches without inspecting bark for signs of
woodpeckers, walk around corners knowing there have been
72 significant bear sightings since March. I'm not saying I'll sleep
inside the circle of mulberry trees, but I'll drink wine made from
any dark fruit. Last June was a melted snow cone of light, sticky
blue & yellow, warm gulf waves & the greenest seaweed I've ever
seen, the heat its own path of thorns. We followed smoked-
tangerine martinis from shore to shore, & when I say *that day*
I mean just yesterday. Somebody was walking down the gravel
road two miles away & we could hear strands of their hair
falling into the dirt when they leaned down to tie their shoe.

The Weekend We Ate Curry

for J.D.

1.

I taught you to Skype, to Facetime, to Zoom, to singe
our words with technology & smudged
screens, the shape of your eyes a surprise through
the two-way mirror, I can't smell you &
I didn't know I needed to smell you:
old grass, mint, toad skin, poached eggs, pineapple,
midnight French toast. The ice here is sharp, gun-
metal bruised, & I was never taught the orange
spells to soften its edges, I carry pink moonstone
in my pocket, send you codes to enter
my video, I clean, I cook, I gather spices & sage
like sacrificial butterflies, unable to migrate.

2.

I bought all the limes today all the limes every lime
this lime & that lime & traveled from store to store &
walked past the lemon bin although I craved the sour
sunshine & color of my mother & the way she filled
my room with yellow blooms & I gathered every lime
in this muddy city & filled my purple arms & repurposed
bags & drove past the Mississippi & ancient burial mounds &
cornfields & sunflower farms & vegetable stands & railroad
tracks & railroad bars & my heart was filled with green &
green & green again & hear this song & I will keep limes in my
mountain home & you will follow the green hum to my front door.

3.

I was up before the dogs, before my tongue begged for coffee, the
streetlights still scattering white drops across wet leaves & fireflies
& frogs, cutting chicken thighs & apples & onions & the cleanest
new potatoes, weeping as I scraped their stubborn skin, before the
3rd shift returned home, before headlamps rounded the corner, a
parade of steal-drunk workers, before you abandoned your rented
bed in Tennessee I was up, I was stirring & stewing & preparing to
drown & the curry powder was yellow & sticky like dandelion
death, like tears of winter wheat, like the postcard that arrived
a year too late with my name, only my name, & no return address.

Who's Keeping Track of Our Dreams

You are chopping hard boiled eggs on Friday night while we
discuss our certain sudden extinction, the vanishing whippoorwill
and his mournful morning chant, our clocks blinking midnight
because tornadoes serenaded our flooded streets. You sold gilt-
edged bibles in North Carolina in 1973 when I was just a child
listening to *The Night the Lights Went Out in Georgia* and
Playground in My Mind, unable to separate those revolutionary
messages. You prop up your broken laptop with a syrupy bottle of
Southern Comfort retrieved from basement waters, still sticky with
mold and spider webs, while we try to mix the ancient recipes:
Comfort Colada, Comfort-On-The Rocks. Our ears popping from
the journey, landing your least favorite part. We haven't been
in Kentucky for twenty-five years, but you never forgot
the flies that laid their eggs on mash, how you waved them
off, wings as black as Mississippi dirt, as green as Irish grass.

I've Been Dead Since the Beginning

I will not consult the Ouija board today, the sun is brittle,
carnivorous, I know what the spirits will say, their ectoplasmic
fingertips guiding the planchette due south, 500 miles

as the crow flies, the tarot cards also will not speak of Spring,
warning me of the usual plagues: locusts, frogs, the
transubstantiation of vodka to blood, unwanted departures,

shedding my seven-year skin, checking the batteries in each smoke
detector, unplugging all electronic devices. The gaping toothless
trunk of your well-traveled car is filled with everyday dishes, what

remains of white plates you removed from your childhood home
after your mother's heart failed to rally one more time. I will not
speak the language of archangels, of snakes, of every poisoned

child, I know my future without the trappings of ghosts, walking
through dead cornfields, black bird swarms, dark tornadoes of
feather, of beak, the wounds you cannot see. The government does

not believe that I am dangerous, my silver-haired portrait causes no
alarm, no photos of my metamorphosis, my open burning eyes as I
peeled six layers of gauze one ruined piece at a time to hold my

scar, nestle it like an egg yolk in my hand and question my own
willingness to let a man with a scalpel and needle do his necessary
work on me. I wake on this sofa that carries the dreams of

grandmothers & revolutionaries in equal measure, two cats, my
hungry familiars, with mirror-image markings of snow-white
blood-black, the sun bares its teeth. I will not look into the crystal

ball today, the porcelain teacup, the old abandoned well to see my
vile moments of ash and self-murder catching up with me.

Devotion

Elegy with Scrambled Eggs

When I say breakfast, I mean your hard-boiled
bruises draped in designer silk blouses,
I mean my first lacy bra, party dressing
in my grandmother's bedroom, the way you
led me to my reflection, your lipstick
mouth saying *beautiful,* I mean you kept
your face in shadow at every meal,
I mean you starved after your husband died
of cancer, I mean you were light headed
for 20 years, I mean the boarding house
where your mother steeped tea on a hot plate,
carried a globe lamp from Baltimore
to Greensboro, I mean the way you claimed
it as payment for the year she left you
behind, I mean the oncoming food truck
that crushed you as you turned into the church
parking lot. When I say church, I mean prayers
to a breathing machine, the way you limped
from bed, re-breaking your ankles, I mean
the last thing you said, *I just don't feel good,*
I mean your hungry children dusting for
unfound fingerprints, I mean pancakes
in the common room on Easter Sunday,
the men who came every week to see you
pour coffee, listen to your hymnal voice.

I mean the choirs in your battered heart
as God set a full table before you.

The Things You Survived Before You Were Born

I cannot explain why you were born on the day the white
cat died, why your lungs were not ready to enter this earth's

heavy atmosphere, cannot help but wonder if your paths
crossed, if you saw his ghost glide down hospital halls

while the doctor raised clean scalpel to release you from
a blood-salt womb. I cannot explain why your sister is not

sitting at home on the yard-sale sofa, waiting to shout your
arrival to the family next door, dodge gutted cars and dead

washing machines to say your name like a sprouting seed
on her tongue. I cannot explain why your great-grandfathers

are lost, one to the grave, one to the orange-winged vines
in his brain, why he will forget you are alive, hear it as a surprise

for the rest of his life, raising photos of you and your brothers
to his liquid brown eyes, shimmering like God's voice, and ask

me if that is your mother. I cannot explain how you rose from
mud-fog into sun, or why I will not sleep tonight without

his claws testing the limits of my skin.

My Grandson Smells of Strawberries

This is the boy who survived. His feet in dirt each day. His eyes on new white flowers & ears on hungry birds. The birds say boy. Fly boy fly. He flaps his green arms & lifts off the earth. The frogs say boy. Here is the juicy swamp. Eat this fly & feel its wings flutter on your teeth. He swims in mud & hugs the worms. The lemon tree says boy. Yellow. But he cannot root & still. He whispers & the snakes think he is their own. They say boy. Wrap us in cotton & clover. Keep us warm through the hurricane nights. My grandson smells of azaleas in winter. Fire ants & mint. Stars & dust. He glimmers as he sleeps.

Fortune Teller

After my 3rd abortion the doctor told me that I would never
have children, don't worry about birth control or diapers,
that's not in your future. You will not be in a kitchen every
night peeling potatoes while a flock of children go from room
to room. Leaving fingerprints. Overturning furniture. Flushing
crayons down the toilet. Not for you the life of folding clothes
with grape juice stains that never wash out or staying up all night
with a fevered child who is so delirious that she imitates Elvis
Presley while you wipe the vomit from her chin. Instead you
will live on the moors with howling wolves and border collies
and 500 wooly animals. You will never sleep. You will never wake.
Your dead babies will call to you like the sheep when a predator
is near, high pitched and insistent and trying to stay alive.

Tea Leaves and AI

There are no deliberate clocks inside
my house, ornate hands pointing to numbers,
eleven as eggs benedict or were-
wolf moors depending on your allegiance,
A or P M. The television keeps
track behind its two-way screen, flashing mid-
night in fluorescent green like it's 19-
79, which it might be, I don't
know, my coffee maker knows, I never
re-adjusted its hours according
to daylight savings, fearful of pressing
any button other than brew, my need
for bleak bitter liquid on my slow tongue
so great I dare not question the machine.

My microwave also stores some record
of changing tides, the angry moon, dying
eggs trapped inside my muted ovaries,
my cell phone and computer both insist
I walk the plank, eyes forward, ignoring
the pelicans who live in an endless
oval of dive and swallow. Loud shrinking
shadows on my deck, the way squirrels grow fat
or die on the pine needle nest. Buzzards
on the highways edge as large as newborn
crones, brake lights like the blood trail my father
left two nights ago when he walked, dreaming,
into an edge, returned to my mother
in their 67-year-old bed, said

I feel so lost. Like me he can't recite
the date without a question mark falling
from his mouth, and I mark the passing days
with the maps he drew for me when I could

not translate inches into miles, photos
of our last road trip, evidence that he
once owned our journey. My receding gum-
line, the decayed state of each remaining
tooth, soft needlepoint of skin, dead lovers
who never knock on my door, the silence
that wakes me, crying for time, tornadoes,
cold babies, red sirens, trains, the yardstick
on my parent's cellar floor that measures
their backwards growth into the hungry mud.

In Which I Compare My Monolingualism to Una Puerta

for Vicky

You tell me you counted my toes, *uno*
a diez, in a language I never
learned. This is not my memory. This is
the sound of your memory recounted
for 55 years, you studied my face,
like a message in a bottle you threw
into a parallel ocean, this is
not my memory. This is the smudging
of your memory, ink on your fingers,
the origami, the prayer, *te amo.*
I sat in fields of shells, prehistory
branded my skin, I collected conches
that my father returned to the shore's edge
while I slept without your lost promises.

When I wake without your lost promises
you tell me you fed me, not with your breast
but with glass bottle, sugared milk, whispered
lullabies that you gave to your other
daughters, the ones you carried home to stay.
This is not my memory. This is cold
and easily bruised, my taste buds never
attuned to your skin, my voice unable
to sing *eres mi sol, mi único*
sol. We never walked in fields of monarch
butterflies, or bought me new shoes, we had
no stairs to climb. This is the soft buzzing
of your memory, hard fluorescent lights,
dragonflies behind the opening door.

Dragonflies escape through the open door,
while I grasp your photograph like a lost
letter, I mix vodka, hibiscus gin,
and ice, stir the juniper, the lillet
will rise, I remember *mis queridos
muertos.* You tell me your torn heart dissolved
into the Rocky Mountains, this is not
my memory, this is the hard landscape
of your memory, the road opening
while I exploded in your womb, a small
apocalypse of mitochondrial
design. *You are my sunshine, my only
sunshine,* I try to know your memory,
the language to count my fingers and toes.

In Which I Refuse to Write a Poem on What Should Have Been Your Sixth Birthday

I sleep with grief serum in my stomach
a reverse feeding tube dispensing drops
like sweetened arsenic or hungry love
drops on suburban sidewalks drops in eyes
of mud-worn green and angry blue drops mixed
with thistle paint swirled into half-blooming
forsythia drops into Easter egg
shells discarded by opulent squirrels drops
to reimagine the moment of rough
conception drops into new lovers' ears
as if to loosen wax as if their hearts
were listening drops from glass skyscrapers
conspiring with sleet until both dirty
melt drops into my own mouth to swallow

with whiskey and skin I wake as vessel
full as vessel indistinguishable
from rain from river from ocean from flood

every body of water as stunned desert
dropped from sky and I am drowning in sand

The Longest Day, 2018

i.
don't ask me about days,
where hours go

ii.
each night as I dream bees,
don't bother me

with abacus beads,
the secrets of Stonehenge,

with sundials or iron
weather vanes, I am

displaced from mud,
from earthworms, weeping

early morning complaints
of crows. I fold

like Rachel. I must erase
this place, celebrate

light without fear, ponder
the skin on top of

my hands, sun-browned
and thin, translate

my joints and veins,
gather thick clouds,

lightning into sign language,
sift through

photographs of grandchildren,
the living,

the dead, my heart
multiplying to embrace

my own division, my teeth
are copper, my

blood like turpentine.
I carry my suitcase,

tired flesh like broken
oyster shells or

postcards to ghosts, search
for long-maned

                    werewolf hides. bring me
                    sacred water,

nightmares without clocks
or prayer books

                    a rock to break the hour
                    glass, her sunlit hand

Mid-Summer Fable

A carpenter bee hovers above the patio stairs, blocking our
path, pale wildflowers behind his small wings & rain just
out of our reach. Then one morning the hawk leaves this
particular field, although some time passes before we stop
seeing his shadow, changes in the texture of light unexplainable
until one of us remembers to look up past the tree line where
clouds are congregating. One day I ask if his tail feathers
were thunder gray or rusted wood and we can't find a single
photograph, someone takes a stick & draws wings into the
moss, but we shake our heads in a circle of memory. No I say,
he was bigger than my grandfather's open hands.

Category 4

1.

I heard the storm pass
right over my house, he said, I was
in the bathtub, unaware
of sirens and weather
reports, pronouncements of doom
relayed by pretty television
people. I heard someone
crying, I'm sure
of it, crying and flying while I washed
my feet. There's no basement in this house.
Be safe, I said, be safe and come
back home.

2.

They cut down her tree. Men
with chainsaws and instructions and no
knowledge that she breathed and held
the fluttering light of leaves in her
eyes. It was a new
death, I said, a scar on top
of scars on top of ashes and laughter and her
baby feet pushing off
from my thighs to jump higher. She was
always looking up and away
from the faces that watched
her every move, her hands
held out like a tiny
hitchhiker, waiting
for a ride.

he is the smallest thing he has ever seen

somewhere is dirt, sodden & bright,
       somewhere a seed,
simple & scattered like sawdust in my father's workshop,
not prayer, not parable

somewhere roots & beetles,
a boy walks through gardens, hidden from his brother & bees

is there a word that means pepper in every language,
is it too soon to call it red, or should I let you
say *rojo* say *rouge* say *aka* say yes, too soon
to question

before the garden, the pepper, the seed,
       the night sweating with fear, he is
holding wet pajamas to the warm
grate, a prayer,
his skin also wet, eyes shining like brown mud

there are voices & hands,
in his mouth a shape like copper
       or sawdust or something unplanted,
he has no word for the sound
of his mother, the way she moves like a door

somewhere this child, a row of unnamed life, a beehive, a brother
lost &
longing for water, & all this is bottled,
brought to our table, & my father says eight drops & his brother
says lemon, & then
we will return to the dirt, and then
we will speak of tomatoes

This Small Machine of Flight

A Water Evacuation Is Also Unlikely

Atlanta was a ghost this morning, miles &
miles of wisp & pine. Ectoplasmic heartbeat
unheard. The moon moaning back at its
streets, the sun afraid to cry. The clouds not
clouds but coffins, not weather pattern, but
unfed soul. It hovered & crept along the
path that Sherman burned. Turned its
haunted face to the sky where I flew, like an
unlikely astronaut & I said to my fellow
passengers, look *Atlanta is a ghost* & it
swallowed our plane whole, down into the
dirty red leaves. Down into the marsh where
I am an unusual light. Where I am forever
orange & drowned.

We Know You Have a Choice in Airlines

They'll think we're in shock he said & I
asked, but aren't we? Standing on a tarmac
holding someone else's baby. I'm bleeding
near the exit wound. My body fights
infection, memories of survivors who we
left behind. Nothing left to lie about but yet
we do. Fiction is always easier than truth.
My ugliest scar, remnant of a foot race at an
icy bus stop, might be mistaken for a shark
attack. Drunken brawl with jagged knife.
There is no knotted ring of useless flesh to
mark your useless death. Uncontrolled time
travel blurs every line: love & silence, song
& despair. Life before you & life long after.

If You Are Unable or Unwilling to Perform These Functions

I've seen faces in trees from the day I was
born. Prayer cards & extension cords in the
back of the closet, single earrings blanketed
in dust. Old red wax hibernating in corners
& dead gnats stuck to the shower ceiling. So
I never look up. A man without a phone
wants to talk & the rest of us are playing
word games that are guaranteed to save us
from Alzheimer's but our hearts are still at
risk. A woman swallows 3 tequila shots at
the airport bar, 7 am, our pale Bloody Marys
shrinking in her wake. I touch books at the
newsstand, consider my future. Knowing I
haven't believed in time or tempo for the
last seven years.

To Start the Flow of Oxygen Pull the Mask Towards You

Most nights I don't know what is dripping in the next room. Intermittent & echoed like the weight of her body as she touched glass, trying to reach her mother's smile. Most nights I don't dream because dreaming is memory in a sodden wool cloak. The secret cabinet where ghosts weep. Sticky & insistent, green & gray. Not hollow or willowy, not a lullaby. Most nights the sun slips a knife into the moon's back. I catch its blood in my mouth. Knowing I might choke. Knowing is nothing, it does me no good, most nights. I measure progress by my inner ear song, the tremble of stereocilia. The warning bells pealing from a crow's parched throat.

Safety Information on the Card Located in the Seat in Front of You

The top bricklayer I've got is 62 years old & ready to retire. There is nobody in line to replace him. A lost art. Like bowling. Interior decorating. Earning Girl Scout badges. Nobody gives a shit anymore. It's 10 am and I'm two drinks in. Not gonna watch the news or text my ex. Time to look over my shoulder. Adjust the rear-view mirror. Find a man with construction hands who is not afraid of oil. The occasional vodka fueled song. Happy birthday to me with Pinot Noir & a bubble machine. My admonishments for EKGs fall on stubborn ears. It's the fourth funeral we've been to this year, but old habits are hard to break. Hard to build a different timeline. Hard to love a man if he is going to die tonight while I'm dreaming of hurricanes.

The Nearest Exit May Be Behind You

My father drove into oncoming traffic today, his tangled brain searching for escape. The windows in my apartment are nailed shut. My mother grabbed the steering wheel & course-corrected. Eased them into the church parking lot & called me to say that I was right, she would not renew his license in March. All travel documents revoked, his known world shrinking shard by shard. The maintenance man is puzzled by my request when frost is expected tonight. I need to know I can disappear without need of a front door. Setting off no alarms. Gather my father's coat & shoes, bible & comb. Take him by his hand, & lead him down this blossomed mountain, one new step at a time.

The Captain Has Turned Off the Seatbelt Sign

You leave St. Louis to re-baptize your heart in saltwater pools. Drink thick martinis. Discuss perfumed soap with a local shopkeeper while I unwrap then rewrap my grandmother's hobnail glassware. I cannot bring myself to throw or give away the doilies she crocheted with twine for her wedding day. Every opened drawer a fortune cookie in reverse. These were things I loved & now float in slumber dust, & I have lived here forever. Where she pushed the keys of my childhood piano, arched her back to the silver melody. Looked up & never said what she saw. Where my cat's heart collapsed one night as he followed the sound of her voice.

Your Seat Cushion Can Be Used as a Flotation Device

This is a world where alligators push their scaly nostrils, their prehistoric teeth through ice to breathe. Where my neighbor's baby is a cotton candy fairy tale & when she cries my quiet heart vibrates like harp strings. A victim of radiation positioning. Where slammed doors make me wonder who is coming up the stairs with automatic weapons or crates of spiced lemons. Where stragglers appear. Old women hand-feed lichen & moss to the last herd of caribou. Where a railroad trestle vanishes into weeds. Pulls kudzu & armadillo bones over its spine & tells me to look away. Where the cats recall frozen dirt from yesterday & will not go outside. Where 4am phone calls lurk in my peripheral vision. Someone asks are you awake & sitting down?

If You See Something Say Something

I cannot speak Spanish or honeybee but I
know it is important to tell you the
moonlight is different in New Mexico. Red
& unafraid of scorpions. Cactus bones. The
worshipped sun will return & spark rioting.
I cannot build a hive, nurture lilac & blue
hyacinth. Hypnotize *Apis mellifera.* Steal
their livelihood for my breakfast tea. I walk
across the Mississippi in July without
drowning or gathering circles of river mud.
There are secrets inside every home, brick
or hexagonal wax. Languages I do not sing.
Spaces where I am forever lost &
welcomed: sweet sister.

The Plastic Bag Will Not Fully Inflate

It's true we are counting days, breathing minutes. I'm 2/3 finished with my lavender latte & the heart is still floating. Ghostlike on the surface while you tell me you are on a liquid diet & vodka doesn't count. Old pen-pals haunt your inbox. Angelica in Germany is cleaning house & declares she's too old for this shit. She says John remember that summer. The sunlight was a song on our tongues & we were not sober for six honeyed weeks. When are you coming back my friend? Hurry. We are all dropping like flies.

Please Report All Unattended Bags or Packages

I'm a medical miracle & nobody knows. My hair is silver, that's all they see. My pedicure is 6 months old & I can't recall the scent of polish. Something plum & bitter. My gall bladder & appendix & shavings of my cervix, blackish moles of odd shape & size removed without fanfare, & nobody knows. My left breast vanished, the flesh replaced with questionable ink & tequila. My heart resides on the wall of the missing. 7 years after it went out for a ride. For milk & a cashier's check & never returned. All the posters now yellowed & brittle & used to start fires. My fingerprints do not match my fingerprints.

Remove Your Shoes and Place Them Directly on the X-Ray Belt

City crews are changing out the drainage
pipes between midnight & 4 am, & when I
wake my water will be unsafe, in need of
boil. I walk across these wooden floors &
you say you can hear my steps, like gun fire
or hail. Something hard & dangerous if you
didn't know it was me. This world is filled
with violence & pain, but a hymnal all the
same. Lighting orange tapered candles &
pouring bad wine down the drain. I pray the
river will not escape tonight. I pray while
we sleep, clouds will creep down the
mountain & under my door. Hold me like a
sainted child who saw God's winged eyes &
didn't burn alive.

In the Event of a Loss of Cabin Pressure

Trust the equation, you tell me. The geometry of a praying mantis. Bulging eyes that seem to view its victim in parallel lines. The distance from the tip of my tongue to my left clavicle is perfectly equal to the number of mice skulls at the bottom of our well. The elixir of her saliva long known to be every alchemists' secret ingredient. He traveled to the moon's surface & she was still dead when he returned. You say if you can measure it, weigh it, count its eggs & offspring, foretell the moment & manner of its death, then you are its only god. The mantis is praying to you.

Please Check the Monitors for Your Connecting Flight

Love is a distant ship. A greenish light in
greenish sky but you burst into this room.
You clean your computer camera with
rubbing alcohol so I can see your face as
crisp as autumn rain. My heart is heavy &
unlovely, a thing that lived in dirt. Survived
frost & floods & droughts. Mole highways
& rabbet dens. My heart as weighted dice.
Anchored. Land-mined. I am fogged &
without yellow. Alone in every photograph
except for the crow who greets me every
morning. His wings like black sunshine &
his sharpened voice, lustrous & laughing at
God.

Items May Shift During Takeoff

Something is walking in the woods that I
cannot see. I follow the trail of pink leaves.
Gnats swarm a statue of St. Francis of Assisi
knowing he will cause them no harm. In the
circle, I find a wooden well, for wishes or
curses, like the core of any renaissance. To
be born again. To navigate the labyrinth. If
time is a construct, can it be brought to its
knees by the slightest drop in temperature,
grass sprouting beneath ice? You are asleep
in a room far from here, & cannot save me
from the shadows I hear. Footfall or slither,
the sound is the same. *Tell me your secret
name.* Gravel stained with pink from
bleeding trees. Newborn ghosts follow my
scent like crow wings.

Check Around Your Seat for Any Personal Belongings

There's a jellyfish on my wall. I bought his frame at the flea market. Ripped out inferior art. 3 dollars for the precise shade of blue. He is silent, of course, except at night when he knits. Needles clacking against glass. He wants a scarf, a sweater, a pair of socks with coral reef design. A way to break through. I've sunk deep into my fantasies: coastal storms, incense that never stops burning. I sleep through firework celebrations & endless rotations of Blue Christmas. Elvis & his hips. The party upstairs where my neighbors forget their manners & rain cigarette bones onto my orange azaleas.

Tighten by Pulling the Loose End of the Strap

A possum followed you off the plane,
tucked under a teenager's surly arm. It
never made a sound, never complained
about sweat or popping ears. Content on
steady ground. You arrived on schedule
but waited behind a loud family of
musicians with carry-on instruments &
strange arrangements of words. Nothing
you had heard in all your travels. Each
one wearing white shoes & the baby
singing fairy tales. Waving its dirty bare
feet. The possum was patient, but you
were ready to exit & find your thick
suitcase. Ready for humming air.
Cathead biscuits & hand-crafted
mandolins. Tales of unresolved love that
sit on the tongue like burnt caramel.

Seat Backs and Tray Tables Must Be Returned to Their Upright Position

The human heart drained of blood looks like wax encrusted candy, an albino chalice. A resting place for headlines. Bodies found in a North Dakota barbershop. Husband arrested after pleading for his wife's safe return. In the remains of Atlanta, I met a couple who sold their house & set out on a tour of mass-shootings. Consoling survivors in churches & bars. The back of their RV filled with mops, bleach, funeral card maps. They know their way by the sound of running water. Mid-town diners, the library of St. Mary of the Sacred Heart Elementary School. The top of a Ferris wheel in Wheeling West Virginia. The rivers, high or dry, will lead them to slaughter. They follow, like trout, upstream.

All Passengers Must Carry Their Own Boarding Pass

The blood orange paint in my fingerprint
whorls should make me unidentifiable. Just
for good measure I spit out healthy teeth.
Shave my head & bleach the stubble. I'm
transferring my soul to a new container.
Something with no bendable parts. More
wet wings or scales or gills. Fewer
eyelashes. It's time to leave, one step ahead
of asteroids. Single cell invasive life forms.
Hitchhike my way back to myself without
greyish organs, radioactive fingernails or
blue eyes. Birthdays. Flashlights. Dripping
black holes. Some-where flowing with
song-soaked stars.

Place All Items Larger Than a Cell Phone in a Separate Bin

You will remember the apple stand, so close to the highway that I was afraid to open my door. This is not how I want to die, anticipating elderberry jam & crocheted pickle barrels. But here we are, un-decapitated. Did I tell you today that I loved you when you took my kitchen scissors & cut the frayed edge of your old pajama pants to create something that resembles a straight line. I was reminded that nothing in this life resembles a map. I will remember the green sign that marked the eastern continental divide, the spot where rivers must make a decision. A crossroad for travelers who offer scraps of true love: roadside tomatoes, prayer shawls, unread palms, unwashed feet.

Supplication

Elegy with Frankenstein

When I say murder, I mean the way slugs
are drenched with salt so hostas and tulips
can bloom, I mean the way your brother dreams
your final face, folded into sofa
cushions for 13 hours until someone
turned you over, I mean purple and red
as metaphor for *livor mortis,* the way
you slapped me when you were eight so I'd save
you from monsters but all I could see was
your sharp handprint on my cheek, I mean green
beans spit from your laughing mouth. When I say
laughing mouth, I mean tears pooling beneath
my sea-otter heart, I mean abalones
on my belly, I mean clean needles as
a metaphor for love, all your tattoos
bleeding ink and pus because you wanted
to paint over every mistake, I mean
the way you stole vodka from my freezer
and I never said a word, I mean your
scattered parts stitched together with chewing
gum and twine and the lyrics of *Let it Be.*

Apollo 11

The carnivorous ground would not suffice
as holy vessel, for all that scattered,
a gluttonous swell of hibernating
earth worms and river toads, the mud itself
an unwelcome choir, this could not be true:
her toes now anonymous white ember,
her legs indistinguishable from skull
fragments, her new soul pitched to seraphic
decibels outside of human longing.
I woke up gnawing at my lonely wrist
to find her in my DNA, entwined
in muscle and bone, drowned in my creaking
blood, like lost rabbits who could not escape
winter floods. You ask me why Forensic

Files, CSI, Criminal Minds, St. Jude
phone-athon, nightly news with lampshade sewn
from human flesh, I say she has no rock,
no flowered scar, I don't know where she's gone,
that I am a connoisseur of disease,
of intricate violent encounters, flocks
of sparrows, murders of crows who whisper
my secret name when I skate the frozen
road, of Neil Armstrong's first daughter destroyed
by a rare and tentacled and brutal
form of cancer, and I do not question
what he saw when he stepped onto the moon.
She wasn't there, I say, not anywhere
in the miles of indecipherable

space, he returned to ocean, to tarred earth,
never in the stars did he find her face.

Hungover Sonnet: Valentine's Day

It started with $4 martinis,
with the frozen ocean bringing you home,
with a starved realization that Wednesday
is good as any to swaddle my nerve
endings with whiskey, morning will arrive
in my cold mouth one way or another,
it started with the ninth funeral mass,
another baby who slept and awoke
outside his body so new that the skull
bones had not linked and locked, with a phone call,
my son's voices returned, living shadows
with copper bones, he tells me *talk louder,*
with vodka in the second glass, April
snowstorm, with hawks that could easily spot
nestling rabbits against the white-wrapped dirt,
with my car dead on the highway as if
to say, *this is journey's ends,* with blood salt,
with hibiscus gin in the third glass, with
a swelling in my uterus, the way
I divided once a month into three
better women, the butcher, the baker,
the candlestick maker, a trail of nail
clippings that even the hamster would not
swallow, with the muddy Mississippi
crawling onto dry ground, circumventing
sandbags, slate, steel, it started with the fourth
glass, with honey mescal and lime, waiting
for you to pull the carpet from its roots.

21st Century Omniverse Sonnet

When physicists in Oak Ridge swung the door
wide to glimpse the negative of narrow
existence, a snail with wet wings emerged,
leaving a contrail, and then hummingbirds,
sluggish and attracted only to shades
of white, and called by metaphysical
choirs to reunite with God and my
father appeared, his oiled brain in clockwork
order, to decode triangulations
of weeping willow funerals, lightning
bugs and vanishing tar pits, but did not
know my face, my doppelgänger long drowned

in mud waters and no one through either
mirror knows if it was an accident.

The Moment Before

I'm sorry to say that you were inside when the sun finally
found my spine. Mixing flour with creek water.
I climbed a tree to find the abandoned starling nest. Or maybe
it was a wren
in a flowerpot beneath the stairs.
A coyote scratched at the door. You were humming and peeling
peaches. I know I am safe with you.
If I had eaten the cobbler before clouds appeared,
I might have brought you the morning dew on my tongue.
The bees were once larvae and now spin my eyelashes into honey.

Ours Was a Softer Kind of Landing

We believed this landscape would not betray,
cinematic sunsets haloing white
farmhouse and cornstalks, as tall as young
men, your cats running free across the road
and back without daylight danger, always
returning home before coyote hour,
high winds that cause old branches to grumble,
the haunted oak tree breaking your bedroom
window, its veined hands reaching for your throat
only to discover that you had fled
to the basement, your nerves frayed, uneasy
at the ribbons of rain that wrapped around
every stone or brick within your line
of sight. I tell you that the wilderness
reclaimed Ukrainian suburbia
after the Chernobyl meltdown, pregnant
foxes and winter wolves roam without fear,
that genetically modified soybean
exhibits natural immunities
to radioactive dirt, that thunder
heads and tornadoes have become common
topics of conversation, that I know
how to hide arsenic poisoning from
the forensic detectives in Osage,
MO but would be indicted in New
Orleans for the same crime. Beige homes destroy
our last corner of beauty and I am
leaving for the Smoky Mountains, this last
sanctuary now coated with poor-grade
cement, the once gentle road a gauntlet
for domesticated mammals, wild skunks,

afternoons of relaxation removed
with top soil. You know that I am waiting
for the next disaster as I hold my
grandson's blooming hand, guiding him around
an abandoned porch in a sweet circle
of splintered flight, that I no longer trust
meteorologists, pretty prophets
with ugly news, I scan the horizon
searching for God's eyes, a voice louder than
schoolyard gunfire, a promise that this
caterpillar boy will wake tomorrow.

Garbage

My body is migrating for winter, following the cranberry trail
of monarch butterflies, the crows eat baby rabbits, unable to resist.
Winter squirrels are building a nest of regurgitated mulberries, full-
ripe acorns, spindly dandelion stems in the back corner of my
deck. Recent-born mice swim in the fermented mix, enter my soft
bedroom. My cat finds their tails, leads them to death by broken
heart, their perfect half-formed bodies drowned in feline saliva.

Samsonite Sonnets

Your last day in Mississippi you threw
the red dishes out the door, frames without
pictures, candlesticks, hand mirrors and soap
dishes, lifeless computer monitors
from 1995, the ocean green
martini glasses your second cousin
gave you after her divorce, pirate ships
in bottles, moon rocks and pressed flowers, fish
bowls and Venetian Christmas ornaments,
anything that would shatter or scatter
like visions of your mother at the sink
with a coconut, breaking it open
to let milk and fruit, like white grains of sand,
spill through her fingers and into the bowl

to make a sweet, perfect cake, and you wept
like a willow tree at every shard
glittering beneath the hard summer sun,
neighbors circling like ravens, dark sirens
in the distance, you filled a plastic cup
with rum and closed the front door behind you,
buried the key beneath dead petunias
and drove north to cornfields and new rivers
and a furnace that would smoke that winter,
waking you from the old dream, your mother
in her burial dress, face painted like
it never was in life, pale pink lipstick,
she dropped your suitcase at the crossroads, cracked
blue, and heavy as a tired baby.

My Friend Is on Fire, Her House Is Ash

She says she doesn't mind. Last month
her son punched her ribs just below her
heart when she failed to cook macaroni
to the consistency that makes his teeth
hum like rain. Last year it was a knife
one inch away from the artery that would
leave her bleeding out on newly washed
sheets. Her other son awake, waiting his
turn. She prays to the hairline fracture
like a line of sandbags to hold back
God's disappointment. She dreams of
distant shores. Of rain. If she melts with
waxflowers, nobody will put him in
shackles. Lock him in a room without
oxygen or bread or sky. If she burns,
nobody will say murder.

The Summer of Foxes

Before it was over, I made my mother cry, mid-September
as the heat was lifting its mossy veil, I was demanding answers,
saying for the third time *he walked into the fire station & handed
them a map.* My children scattered like cicada wings & I not
asking them to return. But no, I made her cry two years after we
found rabbit carcasses in our front yard, two years after our
headlights revealed them walking in an unhurried line against the
edge of our neighbor's house. I made my mother cry six years
after the summer my father built three rooms in our basement,
drove 10 hours home without asking for directions & carved
birdhouse earrings from cherry wood. My children were afraid:
swarms of bats that followed swarms of mosquitos, the way their
grandfather could lift 2x4s above his head, mud wasps & pool
parties, my shrill & desperate voice, their grandmother's tears,
four bright pairs of eyes shrieking back at us across the grass.

Summer Solstice 2016

I'm writing this poem for you although
I don't want to write anymore. I don't
want to drink Bloody Mary's while waves
pull at my feet, I don't want to go dancing.
I don't want to fall in love again, not ever.

The white noise in my head is loud
today, and jagged. The news is full
of dead babies: locked in hot cars, fallen
to the bottom of pools, dragged
back to heaven in the jaws of an alligator.

You are on an island, cushioned
from the sun by SPF 45 and an orange-
striped umbrella. Your heart needs
no protection. The ocean repeats
its chorus like the angels at heaven's gate.

When you read this you will be back
on the main land with pink skin despite
all your efforts. With sand in your shoes,
with shells in your pockets. With waves
of sunshine, JD, with nothing but good news.

Orison

Elegy with Cover Band

When I say music, I mean tornado
sirens on Christmas Eve, the Santa hat
you gave me backstage, I mean the way you
left your bass guitar propped against the wall
after ten tequila shots, I mean multi-
colored women's shoes manufactured
in China, I mean Chapter 11
as metaphor for middle-aged despair,
the way I re-imagined your palm lines
to erase your lack of formal college
education, I mean the day we met
in small town sunshine as a haunted song
you never recorded, I mean *Gimme
Shelter* and lightning and high winds that kept
me on the dance floor until the April
storm passed. When I say storm, I mean the way
your widow ripped white carpet from its roots,
I mean rented death doves escaping
into the Midwest sky like sweet champagne
bubbles while we lowered your mute ashes
into the happy ground, I mean your boss
screaming through phone lines because sales were down
the first quarter, I mean your deep laughter
at Jim Carey in Doc Martens and pink
tutu, I mean the coroner's statement
that you did not suffer, I mean the way
we threw that official report onto
the funeral pyre because we knew

that your heart was large and floating, I mean
the way we always knew it would explode.

I Paint Your Portrait But, on the Canvas, a Library

for C.T.

I ask you for one word, the name of the last thing I loved
with my hands, so hungry and permanent that my fingernails

have not recovered, a way to document *drowning* without
irony, to tell my family that I did not survive the flooded

streets, my bones will arrive wrapped in marsh marigold,
but I am still alive. You send me a hand-drawn map, identify

the point of conflux, provide the original name of each source
of water. This is the last gasp of summer, I say, and you are a

dictionary of each season, the hour when oak leaves will begin
to drop, an index of color, based upon inches of rainfall in April

and May. I mix prairie wolf fur, yellow fire, purple cattail dust,
I stroke your face onto the empty white where I am un-surprised

to see that both your eyes are open and wet, a quiet blooming
of jewelweed at the river's edge.

Tennessee Book of Prayer

1. if you are cooking bacon it must be morning

   spiders nest between the tires of my car & translucent dragonflies shadow our coffee, now shape, now dream, counting birdsong, naming each sound, I say broken-hearted raven, you say the eggs are ready & we are out of salt, drown them in pepper, that's water I say, down the hill, sighing its daily prayer, maybe snakes, maybe it will rain before we close the windows, this is where wasps live in mud or paper or beneath your chair, that buzz is not a wood saw, not a man-made thing

2. this is where wasps live in mud or paper or beneath your chair

   one day I forgot that birds can fly, these unsurprising wings, these breathing bodies in the sky, lost feathers beneath my feet, tucked behind St. Francis, robin with earth worm looks through my window, she is walking on clover, the new rabbits have never seen her underbelly, they don't know what she is capable of, hawk shadow, dog shadow, the scent of human children, all flap- armed & hungry, still believing when they leap off the roof, the sheet will blossom with angels

3. hawk shadow, dog shadow, the scent of human children

   sunday school fingers building God's eyes from penny yarn & popsicle sticks, yellow as mud, green without electricity, I say I am learning to live with spiders, their numerous legs crawling into my dream, fear is a sin, it has no place between rows of tomatoes & wisteria vines, one day the road opened while I was driving to see you, I fell through asphalt & hot tar & landed in a web of high-tensile silk, one day I smelled a swarm of hungry locusts & would not leave my home

4. between rows of tomatoes & wisteria vines

   tonight I'll dance, fireflies on my feet, sun-shined &
   spillway, I'll dance the small lives of garter snakes, the last
   magnolia bloom dropped onto the gravel road, a rooster
   crows all day & I'll dance his restless voice, stones & fool's
   gold at the driveway's edge, tadpoles rising to the light, &
   your face across the room, I'll dance your cold feet swaddled
   in a white blanket, ceiling fan's twirl, I'll sleep inside my
   body, & follow a watery prayer down to the banks of
   conasauga creek.

In Which I Am Surprised to Find Myself in April Again

This spring I am required to turn the tap left, ending the river of
recycled tears, I am required to pray to living children, to their

knees and small stomachs, their throats and green toes, I am
required to cover the witch's well with cut cedar, board it up with

magic mirrors buried beneath the bones, I am required to float
with my grandson in sun-blue pool water, his unscarred skin so

gentle a sponge for all things clean and in flight, his good hands in
motion, his fingers antennae, his voice as deep as a baby bullfrog,

creaky as a rusted bell, I am required to look into the face of my
newborn granddaughter, her crystal ball eyes revealing her amber-

scented future with 90 years of hurricane survival stories, not the
weedy-trailed paths of the past, snakes tasting her heels as she

passes, this spring I am required to take a lover, let something
touch my skin that was born in floods of blood and womb-water

not wool-woven or cast iron, I am required to use my body, remove
it from the cellar where it hides with canned okra, mulberry jam, I

am required to drape it around my songs. I am required to pinch
and be pinched, to bruise, to slither, to goosebump, to wander with

memories of tongues and teeth, to wallow in muddy creeks with
tadpoles and crawfish, I am required to dry myself with forsythia

and dandelion dust, until I am aglow with yellow.

Inside Out Abecedarian

Magic mirror on the wall don't speak,
not now when my face is unfolding like tired
origami. Outside, robins are breathing easier.
Preening. Packs of rabbits emerge from grass,
quietly. Quoting St. Francis, this circle of tails +
revolution + raindrops: I say forgive us I say,
stay, stay. You can't hear behind your glass:
that's treefrogs singing. And bull frogs
unearthed, ugly and croaking hymns.
Valium? Verily? The creek is drowning my
words. Without them I am as ordinary as death.
Xtinct. Xtinguished. Yes, I'm losing letters.

Yes, you too. Until the body count is
zero, zero is all we can ask for.

Listen lovely world I miss you. My days
kite-less. Kitchens have become cinnamon
journeys, jails have become morgues.
Inside, imagining oceans in my ears,
helpless hallelujahs swallowed by gulls.
God goes here.
Fireflies + felons tucked inside his pocket,
every elusive prayer climbing cherry trees.
Dying doesn't scare me. Dimes-stores & daises.
Chamomile cicadas chimes & crossword puzzles.
Birdhouses. Behind my glass I sing *row the boat
ashore.* All I have is this: this is everything.

Around the Table

I need a drink Dale says and reaches for the Pinot
Noir that we bought him just for the occasion
of his friend's expected and breathtaking
leap into the unknown. That's crap, he says,
he killed himself, it's not poetic. Tragic, we say,
I'm so sorry, we say, and move onto the task
at hand. God and prayers and stuff
like that. Lisa's hair is shining and I can't
write a word about her pain. Nouns and verbs
as weak as dying children. You are so
beautiful I want to say but instead I leave it
on the page. Look, it's just flesh, if Monet
was painting your life, your breasts would be
cornflower blue smears on a canvass larger
than this room. We all see the light surrounding
your body. The kitchen is warm and bright. Darkness
scratches at the windows. JD calls for more prayer
and Dale calls for more wine. I'm happy to have both.

Summer Solstice Eve, 2019

There's licorice in the wine tonight and crow feathers,
     Purple Haze on Pandora and I am counting
hours with the underside of my toes, sliding across sanded
     pinewood floors, somewhere my son is counting
his possessions, cataloguing & arranging by size his porcelain
     dolls, tarot cards from largest to small in horizontal
rows, for fear the voices will steal the Queen of Cups.

Tonight, you tell me mescal and asparagus do not mix and hug
     me until I cry, somewhere my daughter is navigating
sprinkler systems and her eyes are my eyes with less moss,
     more ocean gray, black birds and ringed moons,
bloodstone, bismuth crystals & bourbon-soaked cherries as I read
     tea leaves in the shape of whale ribs, dance to Zeppelin
while snake-eyed ghosts insist we walk the hardest path.

Undeterred by baby death, somewhere my youngest child
     is rubbing aloe gel into her birth scars and rescuing
a broken-footed starling, hitchhiking with two children on her
     back to the bird's new home, somewhere I am sleep-
walking across soft carpet, wrought-boned & pale with no poems
     on my tongue, ignoring the buzzing at my window, cedar
smoke, the hard fire that will strip my flammable frame.

Because It's Not the Moon We Love

The way we say it's full like a belly or bucket of water or boil.
How we never say *empty* like toothache but *waning* like evening

cactus flowers before the hummingbirds tongue. I wanted to count
all the moons I have prayed to until I realized it's only one.

Every single thing, rock or raindrop or rosary, carries a lonely howl
inside. I can't remember what the moon looked like the night we

met in a hotel lobby in Columbus Mississippi, but because we are
poets I can say it was circled in pink, with new phlox & cherry

blossoms that congregated at the edge of the Tombigbee just that
morning. Whatever is true, you brought your own satellite, your

lover stroking a small spot on the dark side of your neck. We drank
whiskey. Words like celestial ink drops fell from your mouth and I

wanted a map. I wanted to shred all maps. To row a boat across the
sky, to find your language in comet dust. Or maybe you were a

wayward astronaut and she was the sea where you would crash, the
promise of tulips & hibiscus pie enough to keep you earthbound.

I search for poetry in my dreams while you gather stars above my
home and swallow them. How else can I explain you? I wanted

more whiskey. I wanted more words. You turned your face as if
surfacing for air and she kissed the top of your lip while outside

the moon I never saw sang itself another song about its lovely self.

The Possibility of Journey Is a Heavy Thing

I'm sorry to hear you are filled with dread, that the featureless
voice reciting *One Flew Over the Cuckoo's*
Nest is attached to a bestselling
serial killer, prison-reformed, internet-famous. You confess
that moving from shower to towel, towel
to clothes seems undesirable
today, as treacherous as tsunami water filled with dead
livestock and entire city blocks, the open
road offers you no comfort
with its sudden end, a falling off. The murderer's voice tells you
stories of mothers who lifted school buses
off the backs of their children
and you try to remember those waves of strength, adrenaline-
fueled and fearless, the first time you told
your father no, the day you jumped
from a plane with nothing to drag you back up but nylon.
My realtor friend roars like a lion at breakfast,
while her husband cowers behind
the daily news, nervous about ink on his fingers and the dilemma
of perfect whiteness in the form of a tablecloth
spread before him. She says,
it's all in your head, but I must insist I've never wanted a mansion,
20 rooms flooded with imported rugs, my grand-
mother's salt spoon collection,
large curio cabinets, walnut and oak, like coffins standing on end.
You say, *dread,* I say, tread lightly, with no thoughts
of vanquishing weak and hungry
neighbors, without dusting tabletops, the fear will dissipate, lyrics
left behind in a tangled parachute will return today,
like old prayer or new birds.

Without Church Bells or Sirens

This small machine of prayer, if I die
before I wake, let it be
wet, blue rainwater or melting snow.

Snowbirds storm my dreams, if I wake
before I die, let me be
sharp as a piano, my heart, my torn throat.

Words trapped like birds in my throat, if I sleep
and wake in an empty silo, let me
become stalks of winter wheat or sweet corn.

Let me wake over and over in a field
of orange tulips and ripe cornflowers, I pray
my death is small and quieter than a train.

In Which We are Very Selfish Birds

We are the lucky ones, newly bathed,
towel dried inside this Gulf Coast cottage,
beneath carnivore clouds, our mouths open
to hail & straight-line winds, small tornadoes
that fall from the twisted sky, when these walls
are flattened & shredded like old tax files,
returned to the hungry gods, we will trade
our arms & elbows for sparrow wings, fly
into a lightning bolt's stomach, we will
pass our prayers from beak to beak, feed fledglings
in nests built of plastic straws & paper
money & never think again of droughts
or grasshoppers or remember we spoke
of magnolia petals as evidence
that our love was pure, & our mammal teeth
will transform into violin strings, we
will warble & wail & wake the dead each
morning, we are the lucky ones, we will
not miss electricity or cement,
parking lots or natural history
museums, storm drains or lead pipes, we sang
what needed to be sung, we will shed skin
& bones & shoes, leave the front door open
& drop our keys into the wishing well.

About the Author

Beth Gordon is a poet, mother, and grandmother currently living in Asheville, NC. Her poetry has been published in numerous journals and nominated for Best of the Net, Pushcart Prize, and the Orison Anthology. She is the author of two chapbooks: *Morning Walk with Dead Possum, Breakfast and Parallel Universe* (Animal Heart Press) and *Particularly Dangerous Situation* (Clare Songbird Publishing). She is Managing Editor of *Feral: A Journal of Poetry and Art,* Co-Managing Editor of Animal Heart Press, and Grandma at Femme Salve Books.